Your
Travel
Guide to

ANCIENT
EGYPT

Your

Travel

Guide to

ANCIENT
EGYPT

LERNER PUBLICATIONS COMPANY • MINNEAPOLIS

Designed by: Zachary Marell and Tim Parlin
Edited by: Amy Boland and Martha Kranes
Illustrated by: Tim Parlin
Photo Researched by: Glenn Marier

Lerner Publications Company
A division of Lerner Publishing Group
241 First Avenue North
Minneapolis, MN 55401 U.S.A.

Website address: www.lernerbooks.com

Library of Congress Cataloging-in-Publication Data

Day, Nancy.
    Your travel guide to ancient Egypt / by Nancy Day.
        p.   cm. — (Passport to history)
    Includes bibliographical references and index.
    Summary: Takes readers on a journey back in time in order to experience life in
ancient Egypt, describing clothing, accommodations, foods, local customs,
transportation, a few notable personalities, and more.
    ISBN 0-8225-3075-9 (lib. bdg. : alk. paper)
    1. Egypt—Social life and customs—To 332 B.C.—Juvenile literature. 2. Egypt
Guidebooks—Juvenile literature. [1. Egypt—Social life and customs—To 332
B.C.] I. Title. II. Series.
DT61.D355   2001
932—dc21   99-36810

Manufactured in the United States of America
3 4 5 6 7 8 – JR – 09 08 07 06 05 04

CONTENTS

INTRODUCTION

GETTING STARTED

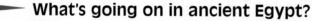

Welcome to Passport to History. You will be traveling through time and space to ancient Egypt. This travel guide will answer questions such as:

- ➤ **What's going on in ancient Egypt?**
- ➤ **What do I wear?**
- ➤ **Who should I meet during my visit?**
- ➤ **How do they get the mummies' brains out through their noses?**

Remember, you are going back in time. Some of the things to which you are accustomed—such as electricity—didn't yet exist. So forget packing your video games, hair dryers, medicines, watches, and other modern conveniences that would make your stay a lot more comfortable. Don't even bother to bring a camera. Cameras didn't exist during the ancient Egyptian civilization, so the pictures in this book are either drawings or photographs made after the invention of photography. But don't worry. The locals do just fine without all of these gadgets and, with a little help from this book, you will too.

The pyramids of Giza, constructed more than four thousand years ago as tombs for ancient pharaohs (kings), greet modern-day visitors to Egypt.

NOTE TO THE TRAVELER

Use this guide as a resource for what to expect during your visit to the ancient Egyptian civilization. The ancient Egyptians left many clues about what life was like in their time. Archaeologists analyze the remains of ancient Egyptian artworks, tools, mummies, and buildings. With this information, historians have pieced together ideas about how the ancient Egyptians may have lived.

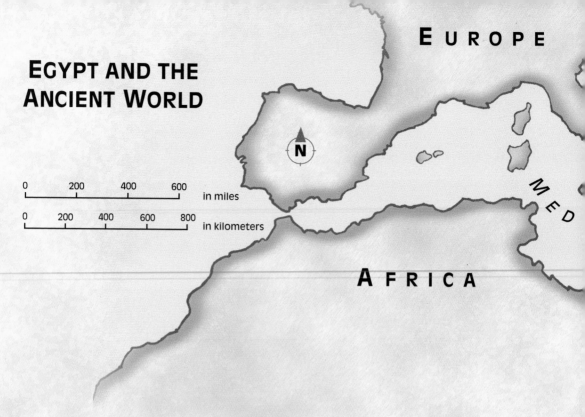

EGYPT AND THE ANCIENT WORLD

E U R O P E

A F R I C A

0   200   400   600
in miles

0   200   400   600   800
in kilometers

Much of our information about ancient Egypt comes from inscriptions in hieroglyphics—a kind of written language using pictures instead of letters. But for many centuries, no one could read these writings. In 1799 the Rosetta Stone, which unlocked the mystery of hieroglyphics, was discovered in a town near the Mediterranean Sea. The stone contained copies of the same message in three languages—hieroglyphic Egyptian; a simpler, commonly used Egyptian script; and Greek, which scholars already knew how to read. The Greek passage helped modern people figure out the meanings of the hieroglyphic characters.

Scientists use modern technologies to understand even more. They examine mummified bodies with X-ray and CT scanning devices to determine their age at death, physical appearance, and medical history. They use chemical analysis to identify substances in ancient medicine jars and cosmetic containers. Studies such as these answer questions about what people's lives were like in ancient Egypt.

Archaeologists continue to make new discoveries. In 1999 a donkey fell through the desert floor into a previously unknown mass tomb that may contain thousands of mummies. Also in 1999, Egyptologists studying inscriptions dating back to 2000 or 1900 B.C. realized the writing was based on an alphabet. While hieroglyphics would have been in use in Egypt for one thousand years by that time, these inscriptions may be the earliest known examples of alphabetic writing.

As new discoveries are made, archaeologists and historians continue to improve their understanding of life in ancient Egypt. Therefore, while this book is a good starting point for your voyage to ancient Egypt, it is always possible that you will find some things are different from what is described here.

WHY VISIT ANCIENT EGYPT?

If you were to ask an ancient Egyptian when a monument was built, you'd get an answer such as, "In the third year of the last king's reign."

Egyptian farmers take advantage of the Nile River to farm the dry landscape. Irrigating fields and directing yearly flooding allows farmers to water thirsty crops.

Egyptians measured time according to how long their rulers stayed in power. Modern people have had to translate ancient Egyptian records to our own system of numbered years. But not everyone agrees on how that should be done. For this reason, you may read different books about ancient Egypt and find various dates for the same events.

Ancient Egypt spans a time period so long as to be almost unimaginable. For example, if you were to visit at the time of King Tutankhamen around 1330 B.C., the pyramids would already be one thousand years old—older than nearly any currently existing historic site in Europe or the United States. For this reason, your impressions of ancient Egypt will vary depending upon when you travel. You may want to visit during the period called the New Kingdom (1539 B.C.–1075 B.C.), one of Egypt's most spectacular eras.

People began to settle along the Nile River in North Africa more than ten thousand years ago. By 4500 B.C., scattered bands of people had developed farming practices, learned to make sophisticated tools and weapons, created artworks, built houses, and begun to trade with one another. They also learned that by cooperating to control the Nile's yearly flood, they could all benefit.

Over time the settlements consolidated into two regions, Upper Egypt and Lower Egypt. Then, around 3000 B.C., Egypt unified under a single king, Menes. He started the first in a long string of dynasties (ruling families). The dynasties created a powerful, lasting Egyptian state.

Modern historians divide Egyptian history after unification into six eras, dated roughly. The Old Kingdom lasted from 2625 B.C. to 2130 B.C. This is when the great pyramids were built. The Old Kingdom was followed by the First Intermediate Period, a time of civil war that lasted until 1980 B.C.

During the Middle Kingdom (1980 B.C.–1630 B.C.), art and culture flourished, trade increased, the military became more organized, and expanded irrigation created thousands of acres of new farmland. Within the Middle Kingdom period, there were four dynasties. Modern scholars consider the Twelfth Dynasty (1938 B.C.–1759 B.C.) to be the classical period of ancient Egypt.

During the Second Intermediate Period (1630 B.C.–1539 B.C.), large numbers of Asian immigrants, later called the Hyksos, settled in northern Egypt. They united and gained political control over some territories. A series of weak Egyptian leaders were unable to maintain central authority, and Egypt fell under Hyksos rule. Meanwhile, Egyptian rulers at Thebes managed to retain control of a narrow strip of land. By the mid-1500s B.C., they had built a powerful army and had driven the Hyksos from power.

The New Kingdom began when Ahmose, ruler of Thebes, took the throne as Egyptian pharaoh (king). During the New Kingdom, Egypt was a major economic and political power not just in Africa, but in Asia as well.

In Upper Nubia, a foreign land to the south, the king of a region called Cush invaded Egypt and established himself as pharaoh, creating a Cushite dynasty that lasted nearly one hundred years. The Cushites ushered in the Third Intermediate Period (1075 B.C.–656 B.C.), and ancient Egypt entered a period of decline.

During the Third Intermediate Period, Egypt's great and far-reaching political power came to an end. A series of internal problems, foreign rulers, and invasions took their toll. Ancient Egypt ended as other cultures—particularly Persian, Greek, and Roman—dramatically influenced and changed Egyptian civilization.

THE BASICS

LOCATION LOWDOWN

Ancient Egypt is a long, thin strip of land along the Nile River in the arid desert of North Africa. If not for the Nile, Egypt would be a desert, too. The locals call the Nile Valley the Black Land. If you look under

In a landscape of rock and sand, lush greenery edges the Nile. Low amounts of moisture and blazing heat make life beyond the Nile unbearable.

your feet, you will see why. The soil along the Nile is rich and dark, ideal for growing crops.

The Nile Valley—the part of Egypt where people live—is only ten miles wide but six hundred miles long. The land around the Nile makes up two very different regions—the Valley, or Upper Egypt, and the Delta, or Lower Egypt. The Valley is a long, narrow area of land to the south. The Delta is a wide triangle-shaped area where the Nile separates into several branches before it enters the Mediterranean Sea to the north.

Upper and Lower Egypt probably have two separate kings until about 3000 B.C., when the two regions unify. After that time, the king wears a double crown made up of the crowns of Upper Egypt and Lower Egypt, and his title includes Lord of Two Lands.

If you visit Egypt between June and October, you will see the Nile spill over its banks during a flood period called the inundation. The inundation doesn't worry the locals because they know the Nile will leave nutrients and moisture behind. As soon as the floodwaters recede, farmers plant seeds in the moist, rich fields. The crops have little need for additional water and will grow until March or April, when they are ready for harvest. After the harvest, the hot sun dries and cracks the ground. You will hear the locals refer to the seasons of the year as Akhet (inundation), Peret (growing), and Shemu (drought).

On both sides of the narrow band of black soil is a desert expanse known as the Red Land. It holds the key to Egypt's wealth and power—gold. It is also a source of copper, which can be made into the tools and weapons that the locals use to build pyramids and expand and defend their land. Gems such as garnets, agates, and jasper; building stone such as marble and granite; and flint for making fire all come from the desert. The miles of inhospitable rock and sand also help to discourage foreign invaders from coming into Egypt.

SIDE TRIP TRIVIA

If you visit nearby Mesopotamia (the area located in what will one day be Iraq), you will find that, like the Egyptians, the Mesopotamians spend a great deal of time trying to manage water. In this case, it's the Euphrates River, which, like the Nile, floods periodically.

CLIMATE

You will find that wherever you travel in ancient Egypt, the sun blazes down from a nearly cloudless sky. If you visit in summer, temperatures will average a toasty 100 degrees. The heat is at its worst near the end of the summer. There is nearly always a wind from the north, which helps make the heat more bearable during the day. You will find, however, that

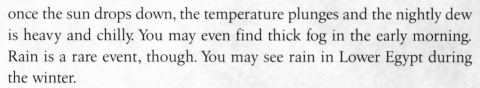

Back TO THE FUTURE

The dryness of the climate helps preserve artifacts, documents, and even human bodies. Modern archaeologists have plenty of evidence to examine and learn a great deal about the ancient Egyptian culture. Much less is known about the ancient Maya, for example, because the climate in Mexico and Central America is so humid that almost everything except stone rots away.

once the sun drops down, the temperature plunges and the nightly dew is heavy and chilly. You may even find thick fog in the early morning. Rain is a rare event, though. You may see rain in Lower Egypt during the winter.

Winter temperatures are milder, averaging 65 degrees. You may want to avoid traveling in the spring, when the weather worsens and dust storms blow in from the desert.

LOCAL TIME

The official calendar started about 2900 B.C. It is similar to what you use at home. There are twelve months of thirty days each plus an extra five-day period to bring the year to 365 days. There is no leap year, even though the locals know that the solar year is 365¼ days long. And without a system for adding those partial days, the seasons slowly get out of whack until winter becomes summer. Summer vacations get really fouled up. Eventually (it takes 1,460 years) this "sliding" calendar works its way completely through the solar year and ends up back where it started. Most regular folks ignore the official calendar—which is used mainly by the government—in favor of the lunar (moon-based) calendar.

The earliest device for telling time is invented by the Egyptians in about 3500 B.C. It is simply a vertical stick that gives a rough idea of the time with its shadow. By the 700s B.C., the Egyptians refine this idea into the sundial *(above)*. A sundial's straight base has a scale with six time divisions. At one end of the base is a crosspiece. When the crosspiece is placed in an east-west position, it casts a shadow that falls on the scale, indicating the time. By 1400 B.C., the Egyptians develope a way to tell time at night or on cloudy days—the water clock. Early water clocks are simply a bucket with a hole near the bottom. As the water slowly drips out, markings on the inside of the bucket show the passage of time.

The lunar calendar consists of three seasons—inundation, growing, and drought. Each season lasts four months. According to this calendar, the year begins when the star Sopdet (Sirius) appears on the horizon just before sunrise. The lunar calendar marks periods of twenty-nine or thirty days from one new moon (the time of month when no moon is visible in the night sky) to the next.

Although there are twenty-four hours in a day here, the actual length of the hour will depend upon the time of year. The locals simply divide the periods of daylight and darkness into twelve sections each. During winter, when there is less daylight, nighttime hours are longer than daytime hours. As the days get longer in spring and summer, so do the hours. This situation would really play havoc with mechanical clocks, but there aren't any, so it doesn't matter. The only clocks you will see are sun clocks and water clocks.

In general, you will find that the locals do not have the same sort of rushing-around attitude as modern folks. They are concerned with time as it relates to the cycles of flooding, growing, and drought, because that is what affects their daily lives.

You will also find almanacs that predict which days are lucky and which days are not, particularly for those born on those days. For example, an almanac may say of one day, "Whoever is born on this day will die of old age." Of another day it may say, "Whoever is born on this day will die of plague."

LANGUAGE LESSON

Few people here can read and write. When they need to send letters, copy texts, create documents, keep inventories, or record transactions, they hire a scribe (a specially trained writer). But as most folks cannot write and cannot afford to pay a scribe to write for them, they rely on travelers for news.

TAKE IT from a Local

Be a scribe! Your body will be sleek, your hand will be soft. You will not flicker like a flame, like one whose body is feeble.
—*from one of the* Miscellanies, *Egyptian books used for teaching*

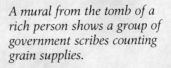

A mural from the tomb of a rich person shows a group of government scribes counting grain supplies.

Egyptian hieroglyphics (symbols) decorate a column of the White Temple, dedicated to the god Min.

The locals value orderly administration and record-keeping, so scribes are highly respected. There are even texts (created by scribes to promote their own profession) that describe every occupation in less than glowing terms (metalworkers stink worse than fish eggs, contractors are dirtier than pigs, teachers are...well, you get the idea).

The bad news is that a student who wants to be a scribe must memorize some seven hundred hieroglyphic signs. The aspiring scribe must also learn hieratic writing—a script that is read from right to left. The locals use hieroglyphics mainly for sacred inscriptions. For documents or private communications, they use hieratic writing. In this system, each picture is changed to a squiggle that only vaguely looks like its hieroglyphic counterpart but is easier and quicker to draw.

If you want to read hieroglyphics, you should know that the symbols are more than just pictures. They are sounds as well. In addition, some signs modify the main sign, changing the meaning. For example, the symbol for "man" next to the symbol for "writing" would mean "scribe." Hieroglyphics can be written in columns or rows, left to right or right to left. If you don't know where to begin, look for a picture of a human or animal. It will face toward the beginning of the line.

THE NAME GAME

The locals choose names carefully, as they believe that the words that make up an individual's name have great meaning and power. Mothers name children at the moment of birth. They choose names that will characterize the person during life and for eternity (in the afterlife). Some names describe the baby's appearance or predict its fate. Others are based upon the cry the mother makes at the moment of birth. An example of such a name is Aneksi, or "She Belongs to Me." The locals

TAKE IT from a Local

If you wish to fit in here, you should choose a name that is similar to the ones the locals use. Try to find one that reflects your personality. Here are some words to choose or combine:

Aha (AH-hah)—fighter

Ahmose (AH-mohs)—the moon is born

Anedjib (ah-NEHD-jihb)—the man with the bold heart

Hotep (HOH-tehp)—is at peace or is grateful

Khasty (KAHS-tee)—foreigner or man of the desert

Ma'at (MAH-aht)—truth or justice

Meretseger (meh-reht-SEH-guhr)—she who loves silence

Miw (MIHW)—little cat

Nefer (NEH-fuhr)—beautiful or handsome

User (OO-suhr)—powerful or mighty

believe that the name generates power every time it is uttered during the person's life.

People's written names are made by combining regular words. To avoid confusion, the locals place a symbol of a seated man or woman at the end to show it is a man's name or a woman's name. Names often include the name of a god. For example, the name Userma'atre means "The justice of Re (the sun god) is powerful." Names of members of the royal family have a cartouche—an oval-shaped frame—instead of the seated man or woman.

WHICH CITIES TO VISIT

Only ruins remain of the ancient Egyptian city Deir el-Medina, which once housed more than one hundred artisans and their families. The people living here were dedicated to constructing and decorating tombs in the nearby Valley of the Kings.

CITY STRUCTURE

Settlements are wedged between farmland (along the river) and desert. Cities are clusters of brick, wood, and reed homes, often surrounded by a thick, high brick wall. Some develop around the estates their residents serve. A few cities are actually planned, with streets and houses laid out, areas for administrative buildings, temples, markets, and so on. But most spread irregularly, according to need and availability of land.

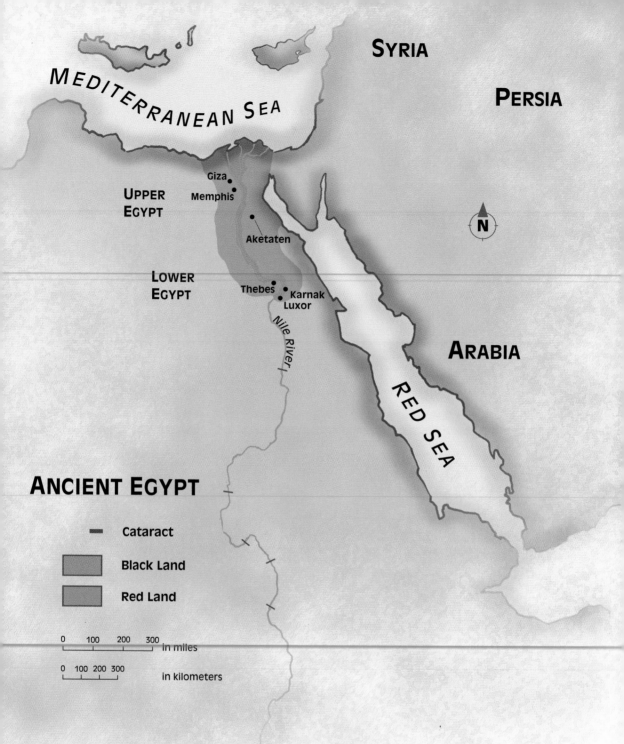

ANCIENT EGYPT

- — Cataract
- Black Land
- Red Land

0	100	200	300	
in miles

| 0 | 100 | 200 | 300 | |
in kilometers

If you walk around a large city, such as Thebes, you will notice the mixed odor of fragrant flowers, incense (a substance burned for its aroma), drying fish, rotting garbage, and burning dung. You will also notice flies—lots of them. In fact, visitors often receive a whisk to keep the flies away. Don't be surprised if you also have to deal with gnats, fleas, and lice. You may even see mice or rats.

You may find it difficult to find your way around without the aid of street signs, newspapers, shop signs, or public notices. None of these exist in ancient Egypt because so few people know how to read. The good news is that there are no advertisements either. To get from place to place, ask a local for directions.

THEBES

If you ask the locals how to get to Thebes, Egypt's capital during the New Kingdom, they will look at you blankly. They know the city as Waset, City of Amun, or simply the City. It is located on the east bank of the Nile in Upper Egypt.

Thebes is a noisy place. Workers are constantly unloading boats filled with treasures for the pharaohs' tombs and stone for building temples and making sculptures. Slaves make bricks from Nile mud, chanting as they work. People jostle through the narrow streets, where the sounds of craftsmen hammering, dogs barking, and children playing echo through the city.

Thebes is where the pharaohs are buried. The locals try to be buried as close as possible to the pharaohs because they count on the pharaohs to take them along into the afterworld. In this way, a necropolis, or city of the dead, has developed around the pharaohs' tombs. Like a city of the living, it has roads and neighborhoods. Instead of homes, however, it has tombs. The necropolis, called the Valley of the Kings, is guarded. You won't be able to see anything but the walls of the cliffs.

TAKE IT from a Local

One comes to port in Thebes. The impious enter not into the Place of Truth. How fortunate he who lands there—he shall become a transfigured being!
—*a writer of the Nineteenth Dynasty*

Don't Miss

. . . the temple that the locals will tell you is dedicated to the gods Amun and Hathor and to the Thutmosid kings. It is actually the temple of Hatshepsut, the woman who dared to be king. The locals know nothing about her because her stepson—who was apparently not pleased to have been kept from the throne for so long—cut out or covered over the writing and pictures on the wall that told her story. Destroying or damaging images of previous rulers is one way new pharaohs wipe the slate clean. Only much later will archaeologists learn about Hatshepsut.

If you visit Thebes, you are bound to see a festival, as the locals celebrate an average of one holy day for every three regular days. There are celebrations to honor various gods, festivals to mark the planting times and the harvests, jubilees to mark the anniversaries of the kings' reigns, and feasts to mark the beginning of the years, the months, and even the half-months. You'll even find that festivals of the necropolis are enjoyed by the living and the dead (so the locals believe).

About two miles from Thebes, you will find Deir el-Medina, the walled village where the tomb makers and their families live. One narrow street splits the village in half. The houses are lined up so closely along the street that, from a distance, Deir el-Medina looks like one long building. The village has no soil or water, and therefore all of its supplies must be brought in from the outside. Even as the workers labor to build lavish tombs for the kings, they build their own tombs in the cemetery just outside the village. The people of Deir el-Medina have their own temple, court, doctor, and even a scorpion charmer.

MEMPHIS

Memphis is a city at the spot where Upper and Lower Egypt meet—the tip of the Delta, near modern-day Cairo. Here the kings reside in their temples and the adoring public comes to pay homage. Depending upon when you visit, Memphis may be called He-ku-Ptah (the Place where the Soul of Ptah Resides) or Yaneb-hej (the City of the White Wall).

These models of Nubian archers were found in a tomb erected during the Middle Kingdom.

If you visit during the Eighteenth Dynasty (1538 B.C.–1292 B.C.), you will find that Memphis serves as a second capital. The city is a political and economic center from which the government controls land and sea routes to Asia. It is the place where troops assemble, workers build ships, and foreign trading vessels unload. As you look around, you will see many kinds of people. Foreign visitors, traders, immigrants, slaves, and hostages all mingle in this city.

NUBIA

Nubia is not a city but a foreign land that borders ancient Egypt to the south, in an area that will one day be Sudan. Nubia is a prosperous land of traders, farmers, craftsmen, and gold miners. The pharaohs of Egypt, wanting to expand their kingdom, set up a series of forts along the Nile to gain a foothold in Nubia. Border clashes are a common occurrence.

In Upper Nubia, the Kingdom of Cush becomes a powerful force, with extensive trade routes and a rich culture. During the New Kingdom, the Egyptians conquer Cush. After this time, you may see Nubians serving in the pharaoh's army or working as servants or slaves.

MONEY MATTERS

Harvesters pack stalks of wheat in a large basket. Since money doesn't exist in ancient Egypt, grain is commonly used to barter (trade) for goods.

A SACK OF GRAIN FOR YOUR THOUGHTS

If you think you have trouble getting your allowance at home, get a load of this—there is no money in ancient Egypt. Copper and gold are common, but no one makes coins out of them. There is even paper (papyrus, that is), but no one makes any bills out of that either. Ancient Egypt is a barter economy—based on trading, not currency.

Workers are generally paid in grain or bread, which they use to feed their families and as barter in the market. If you want to buy something in the marketplace, you must have something to swap. If a merchant doesn't want what you have, he or she will weigh it and set a "price" as determined by its value in silver, gold, copper, or grain. You can trade your item for something of equal worth. The most common measure is a *deben*, about two pounds. For example, a customer may buy a coffin worth 25½ deben of copper by offering animals, grain, or other items whose combined worth adds up to 25½ deben.

Prices

OF COMMON GOODS

1 goat—3 deben of copper

1 pig—5 deben of copper

2 sycamore logs—2 deben of copper

1 tunic—5 deben of copper

1 pair of sandals—1 or 2 deben of copper

1 bed—12 to 25 deben of copper

Daily wage for an ordinary laborer—10 loaves of bread and ⅓ to 2 jugs of beer

Daily wage for a senior official—500 loaves of bread

HANDY MATH FACTS

You will find it easy to catch on to the number system here. It is based on the number ten (like our own system) and is similar to Roman numerals in that you just add the symbols together. Numbers from one to ten are simply indicated by hatch marks (III = 3). The symbol for ten looks like an upside-down letter U. So to make thirteen, you would make an upside-down U followed by three hatch marks. There are also separate symbols for one hundred, one thousand, ten thousand, and so on. Easy, right? There is only one itsy-bitsy problem. With Roman numerals, numbers are determined by subtracting smaller numerals from the larger numerals ahead of them (IX=9). But there is no subtraction in the ancient Egyptian system. So to indicate the number 999, you

A scribe's ruler is marked with ancient Egyptian numerals.

The Egyptians first make paper around 3000 B.C. People collect strips of a thin, membranous material inside papyrus reeds. They beat the strips flat. Then they lay the flattened strips across each other at right angles and press them to create a sheet *(right)*. Finally, they polish the sheet with stones.

need twenty-seven symbols (nine hundreds, nine tens, and nine ones). The symbol for one million is a picture of a guy kneeling and throwing up his hands as if to say, "I can't count any higher!"

If you need to measure size here, all you need is your body. The basic unit of length is the cubit (the distance between the elbow and the tip of the middle finger). The locals also use palm-widths and finger-widths as measurements. Other measurements are a little trickier. If you are purchasing grain, you will need to know that a *hekat* is just over a gallon. Liquids are measured by the *hin* (about one pint).

How to Get Around

By Water

Travel by water is the way to go here. You will travel only during daylight, however, because the Nile is shallow and sandbars lurking under the surface are hard to see at night. Nevertheless, the river acts as a highway up and down the entire length of this narrow country.

You will find a variety of boats, mostly sailboats. The simplest are rafts made from bundles of papyrus reeds. You will also find canoes,

Sailors rely on the wind to power their boats against the strong current of the Nile.

A funeral bark transports a dead body to its final resting place.

ferries, and freighters. One specialized type of boat is the funeral bark, used to transport dead bodies. You can recognize it by its unusual shape—both ends curve up, and the tips are carved to look like papyrus flowers.

Keep in mind that the Nile flows from south to north. Going against the current is very time-consuming, although sailors can take advantage of winds from the Mediterranean. You must also consider whether you are traveling during the inundation. A trip from Thebes to Memphis will take you about two weeks during the inundation. During the season of drought, when the current is much slower, the same trip takes about two months.

During inundation, when the Nile flows across the land, people use boats to cut across the countryside. If you travel in this

IMPORTANT

Safety Tip

Watch out for the stretch of water below Akhetaten. It is lined by steep cliffs, where gusts of wind spin boats toward dangerous sandbars. Huge flocks of birds swoop suddenly out of holes in the cliffs, adding to the terror.

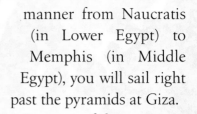

manner from Naucratis (in Lower Egypt) to Memphis (in Middle Egypt), you will sail right past the pyramids at Giza.

Be wary of the cataracts. These are areas of rocky rapids where the water moves so fast that navigation is impossible. The cataracts are south of Thebes, in Nubia. If you plan to travel by boat to that region, you will have to travel overland to get around each cataract.

Travel by sea is even more treacherous and is not recommended for the casual tourist. Ancient Egyptian boats are tiny by modern standards, and much of the time, sailors have no idea where they are. Even experienced locals fear the sea, calling it the Great Green. Nevertheless, they sail to the coast of Syria in western Asia for the wood they need for coffins and furniture. Egyptian boats travel the Red Sea to get incense from Punt in what will one day be Eritrea.

By Land

Most people who have to travel on land use a donkey. You will see horses only if you travel after about 1539 B.C. Horses must be imported and are very expensive, so they are mainly reserved for royal use. You won't see people using camels or buffalo at all.

If you travel away from the Nile Valley, you will have to traverse harsh desert. Most locals fear straying from the security of the Black Land to the dangerous and relentless Red Land that surrounds them. They fear that demons or monsters haunt the desert. Despite the discomfort and the danger, locals travel over the desert to obtain gold, natron, gems, and other important rocks and minerals. They must cross the desert to get to the Red Sea, from which they can set sail on trading expeditions. Travel with an experienced guide, who will be able to find an oasis. Each oasis provides relief from the seemingly endless desert with a small area of pasture and shelter for your animals and a source of fresh water.

Local Customs & Manners

This bust of an ordinary man was carved in 2475 B.C. The ancient Egyptians record many aspects of the daily lives of different people, from nobles to slaves.

What You Can Expect from the Locals

In general, ancient Egyptians are slightly smaller, than people at home. On average, the men are about five feet five inches tall, the women are about five feet. Their skin is brown, their hair is dark, and they look a lot better than the mummies you may have seen.

Although you will not find discrimination based on skin color, you will find that Egyptians view people born elsewhere as barbarians. The locals have an abusive name for virtually every non-Egyptian group.

Kids have it pretty good here—if they survive, that is. Many children die before their fifth birthdays. While they are younger than seven, they do very little other than play. (Boys as young as three, though, may run errands and feed animals.) Children play with tops, dolls, animal figures, puppets, model boats, balls, miniature weapons, and even mechanical toys such as a row of miniature figures that dance up and down when a string is pulled. They keep pets such as birds, cats, and baby gazelles. Kids also enjoy swimming. You will find lots of places for watery entertainment, from garden pools to the Nile itself. After age seven, boys begin to perform more chores. Girls run errands, prepare food, and help care for the livestock. When they are twelve, kids start working in the fields. Both boys and girls baby-sit younger brothers and sisters. Girls as well as boys may go with their fathers on hunting trips.

A man's daughters, wife, and son accompany him on a hunting trip in the marshes of the Nile.

A husband and wife work side by side harvesting wheat.

You may be surprised to find people holding down jobs, marrying, and having children while in their teens. The locals consider a boy of fifteen to be a man. Most boys follow their fathers into business. The pharaoh appoints all the civil, religious, and military officials, so a boy must have the pharaoh's favor to get one of these jobs. Most girls end up with lives similar to their mothers'. They work in the home, bear and raise children, weave cloth to trade at the market, labor in the fields, or perhaps work as singers or dancers at a temple.

Don't expect to see any weddings here. No official ceremony or religious service marks a marriage, although you may see family and friends celebrating with feasting and entertainment. Marriage is a contract between a man (who provides two-thirds of what will become their jointly owned property) and a woman (who supplies one-third). This joint property forms their household. One day they will leave their shared property in equal portions to their children. Although parents sometimes arrange marriages to create ties with another family, people also marry for love. Divorce is common, and people may marry several times.

People here don't expect to live long. Men live, on average, to age thirty-five. Women have a life expectancy of thirty. There are some amazing exceptions, however, such as the pharaoh Ramses II, who lived to nearly ninety.

THE SOCIAL & POLITICAL SCENE

The social structure here is more organized than what you'll find at home. The pharaoh is at the top, followed (in increasingly larger numbers) by nobles, then skilled workers, unskilled workers, and finally peasants. By the late New Kingdom, this population adds up to four or five million—the majority of which are workers and peasants.

The political structure is arranged much the same way, with the pharaoh on top. Government is by the pharaoh's decree (command). Society operates according to the sum total of all these decrees. Decrees often overlap or create confusion. When someone files a complaint about a specific case, the king may issue another decree in response. There is no overall plan or document such as the U.S. Constitution.

The pharaohs are very big on taxes, which people must pay in grains, animals, linens, or other goods. The king's view is that everything belongs to him, so he can tax everything to help support the king-dom. Taxes pay wages, buy rations for workers, and fund building projects, temple maintenance, palace administration, and so on. Taxes also support the lavish royal lifestyle.

As you might imagine, pharaohs lead very different lives from the rest of the locals. They are considered descendants of the gods. Egyptians believe pharaohs will continue to reign in the afterlife. Since the

Queen Nefertiti and King Akhenaton

If you would like to see the pharaoh, try visiting the city of Akhetaten. A covered bridge connects the palace to the royal residence on the other side of the road. In the middle of the bridge, you will see the Window of Appearances—a small room with a balcony. The pharaoh comes here occasionally to see his adoring public and to reward faithful subjects with gold, which he throws from the window.

pharaohs are both political rulers and religious leaders, they govern with the authority of a god. Pharaohs are the supreme religious leaders, serve as commanders-in-chief of the military, and are the ultimate judges in all legal disputes.

Just as kings live very differently from the way common men do, queens live very differently from common women. People highly respect queens, and some queens even have quite a bit of power. Some, such as Nefertiti, rule with their husbands as partners. Tiy, wife of Amenhotep III, issues decrees in her own name and corresponds with foreign rulers. Depending upon when you travel, you might even meet a female king.

A nobleman inspects his livestock.

The nobles at the upper levels of society control most of Egypt's wealth and power. This group includes members of the royal family, priests, administrators, military officials, and scribes. Egypt depends on scribes to oversee and record most government functions.

Another important social group here is the artisans. The pharaoh, priests, and government employ carpenters, bricklayers, sculptors, painters, and other craftspeople to work in tombs. They also use goldsmiths, cabinetmakers, weavers, and other artisans to create works for the royal court. Chariot makers, leather workers, boatbuilders, and other specialists create supplies for the army. Artisans make enough money to live comfortably, and their employers provide them with housing and other benefits.

Peasants, who have to earn their own living by farming and trading at the market, have tougher lives. They are at the mercy of the weather, the rise and fall of the Nile, and their own ability to manage the soil productively. The pharaoh may assign peasants to dig, haul, and do other unskilled work on the tombs during the inundation, when people aren't busy farming.

While these social levels may appear rigid, you will find nobles who also farm, officials who are also coppersmiths, and so forth. People can move up the ladder of social success to a certain degree.

Ancient Egyptian artisans, such as carpenters, brick makers, metalworkers, and stonemasons, work at their crafts.

A woman's status is determined mainly by the social level of her father or husband. If a woman's husband is a farmer, she may work in the fields. If he is a businessman, she may run the business during his absences. Women are full citizens, equal to men in the eyes of the law. They can buy, sell, or rent property and engage in business on their own. Women control one-third of any property they own with their husbands. Wives and daughters can also inherit property in their own names. But Egyptians don't allow women to go to school. Therefore women can't do jobs that require reading, writing, or specialized training. Women usually don't make as much money as men. Many, however, are able to barter their homemade goods (such as woven cloth, baskets, or clothing) in the marketplace, adding to the family's earnings. Women also find work as musicians, boat pilots, perfumers, weavers, beauticians, florists, and even doctors. Some work in mills, breweries, or bakeries, often alongside their husbands.

SLAVERY

You will find many people here own slaves. Even people who are not wealthy may have one or two slaves. Most slaves are foreigners, and many are prisoners of war. But you will also find Egyptian slaves. Male slaves perform heavy labor, work in the fields, or act as servants to their masters. Female slaves perform household tasks. The state owns slaves to staff the temples and perform other jobs, such as digging canals, constructing buildings, and raising dikes (walls) to direct the waters of the Nile. Slaves may also serve in the army or sow and harvest crops. The worst slave work is in the gold and copper mines of the Red Land, where the heat and lack of water create additional hardships.

Slaves can be sold, left as an inheritance, or hired from their owners. They do have some rights. For example, they can own property and marry freeborn people. Slaves who work for the royal family or for nobles often lead more comfortable lives than Egyptian peasants, who have to struggle to survive. Children of royal slaves may learn skills that lead to jobs with the Egyptian government.

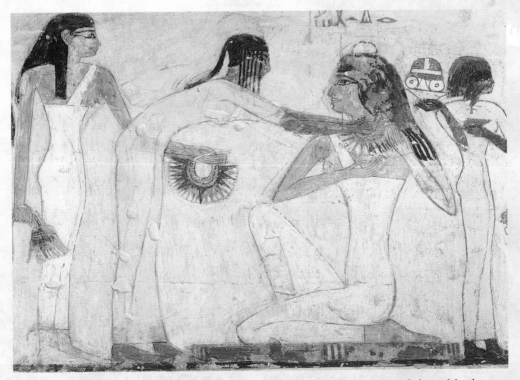

Household servants adorn guests with fragrant flower necklaces and pass dishes of food at a banquet.

The ancient Egyptians believe that Nut, the sky goddess, separates heaven and earth (right). Osiris (below), god of death and fertility, has green skin to represent new life.

LOCAL MANNERS

While you are out and about, you will run into the locals. As you do, you should say, "Welcome in peace!" or, "In peace, in peace."

When you sit down to eat, you will notice that the locals have a ritual similar to saying grace. They bring out a wooden statue of the god Osiris, in the form of a mummy, to remind everyone of his or her own mortality. While guests are encouraged to enjoy themselves, they are also advised to remember that all human pleasures are temporary and that one day the end will come.

Table manners are more relaxed in ancient Egypt than you may be used to at home. The locals wash their hands before meals because they eat with their fingers. If you are served meat, you should hold it in your hand and nibble from the bone. There are no napkins, but don't worry if your fingers get sticky. A servant or a daughter of the household will bring water for washing after the meal.

You may find there is only a single bowl of food in the center of the table. Dip your bread in the dish, taking turns with the other diners.

Save room, however, because at a signal from the host, the servant will remove that dish and serve the next.

LOCAL BELIEFS

The locals see the universe as having four corners—the south (where the Nile begins), the north (where the north star is located), the east (where the sun rises), and the west (where the sun sets). Their concept of the universe is associated with birth, death, and rebirth. The sun god, Re, rises in the east (birth). He ferries across the sky each day in a boat, and then travels through the underworld (death). He emerges in the east each morning to rise again (rebirth).

The locals believe that the sky is made of water. They believe that life on earth exists inside a

Hot Hint

You may hear the locals refer to someone as "Osiris (name)" to note that the person is dead (the way you might say "the late Mary Smith"). By 2040 B.C., the end of the First Intermediate Period, the locals begin to believe that anyone who is buried with the proper prayers and procedures can become one with the body and spirit of Osiris.

bubble made by the atmosphere, which keeps the sky from collapsing onto the earth. They picture the universe as round, and by 350 B.C., they believe the earth is round as well.

When a pharaoh dies, people expect that he will rise into the sky, be transformed into a star and the sun, and then become part of Osiris, the god of the afterlife. Massive tombs and temples guarantee the pharaohs' continuous divinity.

Inside the temples, you will often find columns. Some of these are huge—forty feet tall or larger—and can be nearly half as wide as they are tall. In the hall at the Temple of Amun in Karnak, there are columns

TAKE IT from a Local

Egyptians depict their gods as humans, animals, or a combination of both. The gods also overlap quite a bit, with one taking on the duties of another.

Amun or Amen (ah-MOON)—god of Thebes

Anubis (uh-NOO-buhs)—god of the dead and mummification

Atum (AH-tuhm)—creator god

Geb (GHEHB)—earth god

Hathor (HAH-thuhr)—goddess of love, beauty, and joy

Horus (HOH-ruhs)—son of Osiris and Isis. He rules Egypt through the pharaoh, whom Egyptians consider to be Horus in human form.

Isis (EYE-suhs)—goddess protector of children and of the dead

Ma'at (MAH-aht)—goddess of truth, law, and justice

Osiris (oh-SY-ruhs)—god of the dead and the afterlife

Re (RAY)—sun god

Seshat (SEH-shaht)—goddess of learning

Seth (SEHTH)—god of chaos and storms

Thoth (THOHTH)—god of writing and wisdom

so wide that one hundred kids could stand on the top of one of them. The columns come in different styles, many of which resemble plants.

Don't plan on just walking into a temple as if it were a modern-day church. Ancient Egyptians believe temples are where the gods live. Only the highest priests are allowed into the inner, sacred area of the temple to approach the statue the god inhabits. Ordinary citizens pray to the pharaoh at the temple gate and count on the pharaoh to act as a messenger between the people and the gods.

The shrine that houses the statue of the god is sealed at sundown each day. In the morning, the high priest breaks the seal, lights a torch to wake the god, says prayers, lights incense, washes the statue (which may be solid gold), places fresh clothing and jewels on it, and places offerings of food and drink near it. Singers offer hymns of praise to the god. At the end of the day, the priest backs out of the shrine, sweeping away his footprints as he goes, and seals the sacred area again.

At times, people parade the statues of the gods through town so that the locals may make direct appeals to the gods. They ask specific questions, such as, "Is it he who has stolen my mat?", or general questions about the future, such as, "Are my dreams good?" A scribe writes each question on a small stone and presents it to the statue as it is being carried through the village. The statue is expected to nod or move in answer, creating a pressure its bearers can feel.

The locals also worship at home. Most people have small shrines, which they use to worship not only the major gods but also the gods that might be able to help them in a specific area. For example, a scribe may worship Thoth, the divine scribe and inventor of numbers (do you think it means anything that he is represented by a baboon?).

DEATH & BEYOND

The locals go to great lengths to try to extend life beyond the grave. The funeral and burial customs you see are all geared toward the same goal: to allow people to continue to live after death, with the same social status, comforts, and companions they had when they were alive.

The locals preserve dead bodies through mummification. As with modern funerals, the degree of extravagance is related to the amount of money the relatives are willing to spend. Embalming (body preservation) may consist simply of rinsing the body (most common folk do this). Mid-level social classes can expect embalmers to prepare the deceased person with natron, a chemical that dries the body. Complete mummification, which is most highly developed in the New Kingdom, is expensive and takes a long time. It is usually reserved for pharaohs and the highest social classes.

When a pharaoh or someone of wealth or importance dies, relatives take the body to a special "house of purification" for treatment. A priest with surgical training acts as an embalmer to preserve the body. First he makes a cut in the side of the body and removes all the organs except the heart (the locals believe the heart is where memories are stored). Then the embalmer uses a hook-shaped tool to remove the brain through one of the nostrils.

Next the embalmer covers the entire body with natron and leaves it to dry for up to seventy days. Without moisture, the bacteria that cause

Priests and servants help prepare the dead for burial.

Back TO THE FUTURE

Modern Egyptologists originally thought the ancients used a long, hooked instrument to pull the brain out through the nose. But when mummy expert Bob Brier tried this on a real dead body in 1994, he found he couldn't do it. Instead, he used the instrument to stir up the brain until it was almost a liquid. Then he turned the body upside down and the brain drained out through the nose. So this is probably how the locals do it. Check it out. But not right after lunch.

decay cannot live. The embalmer dries the organs with salts and treats them with oils and melted resin (hardened tree sap).

The embalmer stuffs the dried body with sawdust, ashes, and salt to fill it out. He then either puts the organs in special containers called canopic jars or individually wraps them and puts them back into the body, along with four wax figures representing the guardians of the dead. His last step is to apply cosmetics and artificial hair (even eyebrows). He puts false eyes in the empty sockets to replace the real eyes, which dry

A dead person's organs are placed in canopic jars. Each jar has a protective power. From left to right, the falcon Qebehsenuf guards the intestines, and Duamutef the jackal protects the stomach. Imsety, a human, guards the liver. The baboon Hapi watches over the lungs.

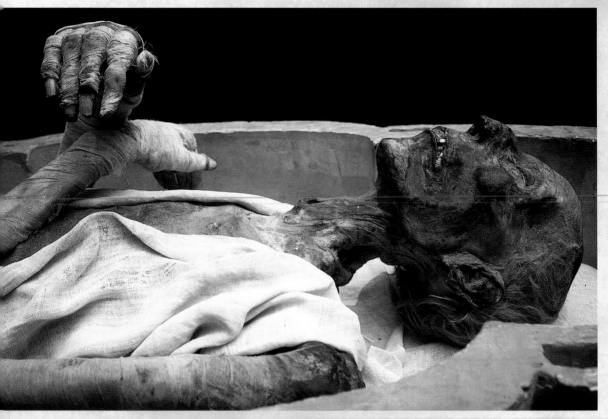

The mummy of Ramses II lies preserved in his coffin.

up during the mummification process. If the person has lost a leg, the embalmer may even equip the mummy with an artificial leg, to assure a whole body in the afterlife. He may also place special charms and decorations on the body for protection and as symbols of life or endurance in the afterworld.

Following instructions from sacred texts, the embalmer wraps the body with strips of cloth that resemble bandages. Then he melts resin and pours it over the wrappings before covering the body with another layer of cloth strips. He continues in this way until the body is a thick, rigid mummy. Before he puts the final layer of wrapping on the body, the embalmer places a funerary mask over the head and shoulders of the body. He then covers it with a special linen sheet decorated with a picture of Osiris, the god of the dead.

The embalmer places the mummified body in a coffin, and he may place that coffin in another coffin. Early coffins are plain wooden boxes, but as time goes on, they get much more elaborate. By the New

Kingdom, there are richly detailed, colorful mummy-shaped caskets. The coffins are then placed inside a sarcophagus (a stone box). The coffins, the sarcophagus, and the walls of the tomb are all covered with religious inscriptions.

The funeral, which only takes place after the body has been mummified, starts with a long procession to the tomb. The mummy is at the front of the line, carried on a large sled pulled by oxen. If you watch one of these processions, you will notice the women are crying and shouting, perhaps even tearing at their clothes. This is an expected part of the mourning process. In fact, the women making the biggest show may well be professional mourners hired to increase the show of grief.

This Egyptian coffin is ornately decorated inside and out.

Behind the mourners, you will see people carrying furniture, food, clothing, jewelry, wigs, cosmetics, and other possessions. These are not for the funeral attendees. The locals believe that people live in the afterlife just as they have lived in this life. Therefore they need the appropriate supplies. It's like packing for a long trip, only more difficult because it is for eternity and the dead person can't just go out and buy anything that has been forgotten.

Before the body is placed in the tomb, dancers perform a ritual dance. Then the mummy is stood up at the opening of the tomb. A priest wearing a leopard skin conducts a special ceremony called the Opening of the Mouth. The locals believe that a person's individual characteristics comprise a spiritual entity called *ba*. Ba must return and breathe life into the mummy through its mouth to give the person back his or her unique character. You may see pictures of ba as a person with the head of a bird. Even more important is the life force, or *ka*, which needs food and a place to reside. The mummified body, a statue, or even a picture

A procession of servants carries furniture to a tomb.

of the dead person can provide the ka with a home. The ka, the ba, and a third entity, the *akh* (the spirit of the dead person that can interact with the living), make up what modern people would call the human soul.

All of the burial rites, from the preservation of the body to the magical symbols and writings on the walls of the tomb, are designed to assure immortality. Because the ka must be fed, family members, servants, or hired priests regularly take food offerings to the tomb. Traditionally, the eldest son is responsible, as part of his inheritance, for the continued nourishment of his deceased father's ka. He may convince his brothers and sisters to help, in return for a share of the inherited property. Some tombs contain a sort of insurance policy—a written message on the walls begging visitors to leave offerings.

As in life, the treatment a poor person gets in death is considerably different. The common Egyptian is not mummified, has no coffin, no tomb, and may not even get any offerings. Relatives simply place the body in a hole in the ground and cover it up. Even the poorest person, however, receives some essentials for the afterlife. The person's relatives will bury him or her with some cosmetics and perfumes, a few possessions (perhaps a simple bracelet and a ring), pottery jars containing food and drink, and tools (needle, cloth, and thread for a seamstress, for example).

The locals envision a passage to eternity that is packed with hazards and challenges. The dead person must know the proper spells and even the underworld names for nearly any piece of wood or stone he or she might encounter. A door bolt, for example, might demand that the dead person give its correct name (Toe of His Mother) before it will open. To help, the locals place a sort of "cheat sheet" in the dead person's tomb. The cheat sheet is the Book of the Dead, a series of texts that provide instructions, advice, and nearly two hundred magical spells to help the person pass successfully through the afterworld.

If the dead person survives the trip through the afterworld, he or she must still face the biggest challenge: final judgment in the Hall of Two Truths. As in a court of law, the dead person faces a judge, a jury of dozens of gods, and witnesses. The dead person must deny a series of charges. Then the gods weigh his or her heart against a feather, the sign of truth. If the heart and feather are in balance, the person's heart contains no deceit and is free to join the sun god and achieve eternal life. If

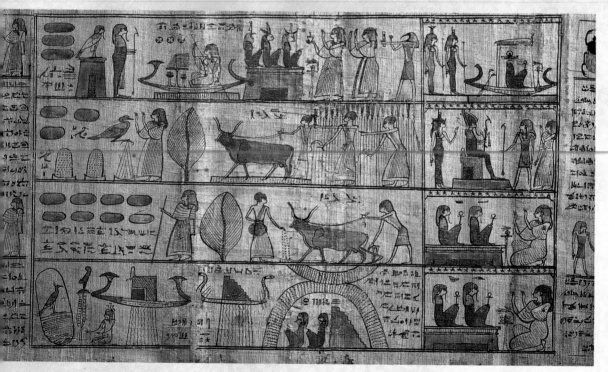

A detail from the Book of the Dead inscribed on papyrus

Osiris oversees the weighing of the heart of a noble.

not, the Swallowing Monster, Ammit (sort of a combination of crocodile, hippopotamus, and lion), devours the heart, leaving the person with no reason, memory, emotion, or personality. This results in a second death, from which there can be no chance for an eternal life in the afterworld.

The locals continue to communicate with friends and family after death. They believe spirits survive death and are still part of the community. They send letters to the dead to ask for help, to make sure the loved one is comfortable in the afterlife, and to ward off bad spirits. Such letters are often written on bowls, which can be filled with offerings. It is also considered good manners to say the name of a dead person when you pass his or her monument—it helps keep the person's memory alive.

WHAT TO WEAR

CLOTHES

The first thing you need to know about clothes in ancient Egypt is that they are optional, particularly for young people and the poor. Because the weather is so hot, the locals think nothing of wearing nothing, or next to nothing. Adult clothing can be quite sheer, and men may skip clothing entirely while hunting or fishing (watch that hook!). Young children generally don't wear any clothing at all unless they are cold. Older children dress like adults.

When people do wear clothes, the styles are plain. The color of choice is white, which is cool in the hot sun. You will see some colorful robes and dresses and some clothes with tassels, colored weavings, or embroidery. Clothing becomes more ornate in later years. By the end of the New Kingdom, you will see showier clothes, oversized jewelry, and massive hairstyles.

Egyptians make most clothing from linen. Cotton and silk have not been discovered yet. You may see woolen outer coats, but Egyptians consider wool ceremonially unclean and feel that it mustn't touch the skin. People wearing wool are not allowed to enter temples, either.

Most men wear a pleated skirt sort of like a kilt. If you look carefully, you will see that the kilt is really just a rectangle of fabric tied around the hips. Some of the ties are quite elaborate. Men may wear a shirt with the kilt, but they often go topless. Shirts are generally plain, collarless, and have wide, pleated sleeves. Men may also wear robes, which are pleated and made from sheer material.

Women wear linen dresses. In the Old Kingdom days, the linen dress is clingy and full-length, with straps that just barely cover the breasts. You may want to add a mantle—a long piece of material that is draped over the shoulders or over one shoulder and under the other arm.

In a segment of a tomb painting in Thebes,
the goddess Hathor and King Sethos I are
shown wearing the fashion of the time.

Ancient Egyptian sandals don't provide much arch support. However, most people go barefoot.

If you visit in later periods, you may find more elaborate dress. On men you will see a pleated skirt and robe complemented with a shoulder-length wig. A common style for women is a long, straight dress that leaves one or both breasts exposed. You will see a pleated robe made from nearly transparent linen that is open all the way down the front but may be tied at the waist with a sash. A short, pleated cape goes over the shoulders and ties in front. You may want to wear something under it, but you will notice that some of the locals do not.

You will find that dress varies by occupation and position. Men and women who labor under the hot sun in the fields may wear only a loin-cloth or short kilt. Viziers (high-ranking officials) wear straight, full-length, unpleated robes with narrow straps that tie around the neck. Sailors wear a leather patch on their seats to reinforce the area that gets the most wear while sitting on a rower's bench.

Most folks here go barefoot, especially the women and children. You will see sandals, however, particularly at important events. Most are made of papyrus or leather. Egyptians wear sandals when working in tombs or other areas where they might step on sharp rock fragments. Wealthy people wear red leather slippers.

Tech Talk

The locals smooth fabric using a flat piece of wood with a handle, or they flatten it by passing it through a series of wooden rods. They achieve more elaborate patterns, such as wavy lines or pleats (pressed folds), by using wooden planks that have impressions cut into them. They lay the fabric on the board and press it to force it into the indentations.

A princess of Amarna wears her hair braided off to one side.

HAIR

Children generally wear their hair long until they reach puberty. Boys shave their heads except for a patch on the top of one side, which they leave long to braid. A boy's sidelock is cut off when he grows up. Girls wear their hair loose, in braided pigtails, or in a style similar to the boys', with the braid rolled into a curl on the right side of the head. Girls may also wear a single braid, perhaps with an ornament hanging from the end. You will see a variety of gold or silver hair decorations, sometimes shaped like fish, with bits of turquoise, carnelian, or other semi-precious stones.

Women have a variety of hairstyles. Some wear their hair long and straight, similar to what you might see at home. Others create many tiny braids, curls, or ringlets. You will see tall, puffy hairstyles, which may be enhanced with artificial hairpieces. Women also dye their hair red with a plant-based dye called henna. You may see men with short hair very much like at home, but many wear their hair longer. One style is a long, blunt cut, similar to the women's style. The style you may have seen in books—short bangs with the rest of the hair long and cut at an angle on each side—is common during the Middle Kingdom.

Hair removal is a common part of personal care here. Men and women often shave all or part of their heads and remove unwanted hair from other parts of their bodies. To remove hair, the locals use hooked bronze razors and tweezers.

Men generally don't have mustaches or beards, but you may see narrow, short beards or small mustaches on both peasants and nobles. Men with beards are among those forbidden to enter temple sanctuaries.

The scribe Amenhotep wears a fashionable wig.

Wigs are very much in demand by both men and women, so feel free to wig out. Wigs are made of real human hair, so they are all dark (no blonds here). They have a pad underneath to allow air circulation. Some women's wigs are as wide as their shoulders. Kings even wear false beards for special ceremonies. Egyptians have remedies for gray hair and baldness for those who prefer their own hair.

BEAUTY

Egyptian women spend quite a bit of time and effort on their faces. Some have whole chests filled with mirrors, cosmetics, tweezers, razors, brushes, and combs. You will find many cosmetic ointments, oils, and scents (saffron oil is a particular favorite). The dry air takes its toll, so you will see many ointments to soften and moisturize the skin. These are scented with flowers, fruits, or herbs, but the main ingredient is fat—from crocodiles, hippos, or even cats. You will also see blush made from red ocher, which can be used on the lips as well as the cheeks.

If you wish to copy the local style, you will need eye paint, which is made of stone crushed into a paste. It is available in green and gray. Use a tiny bone or wooden rod (or your finger) to apply the paint in thick lines over your eyebrows and around your eyes like eyeliner. Use dark gray on your eyebrows and upper eyelids and green on your lower lids. Men, women, and even children use makeup to emphasize their eyes.

You will see a wide variety of jewelry for men as well as women. Some designs are quite simple, but others are very ornate. The well-dressed local might wear earrings, a necklace, bracelets, armbands, rings, and anklets, all at the same time.

Necklaces are particularly common. One favorite style is a wide collar made with strings of beads or stones. Pendant necklaces, which have a large charm hanging from a cord or a gold chain, are also popular. At feasts, you may see necklaces made from live plants or fresh flowers. You will also see bracelets. Some of these are made of beads, and others are solid pieces of copper or gold.

Women here wear earrings, but then so do boys and perhaps men. If you have pierced ears, you will be at an advantage, although be prepared that the posts of some earrings are very large—up to two inches in diameter. There are lots of styles from which to choose, including hoops, dangles, and ear studs.

Don't Miss

. . . local makeup. The locals are the first in history to mix compounds to create perfumes, face powder, and eye shadow.

WHAT TO SEE & DO

SITES TO SEE

As you travel around ancient Egypt taking in the sights, you may meet locals who are sightseeing, too. Just as modern Europeans enjoy looking at medieval castles built in the A.D. 800s or 900s, the locals here tour old temples, pyramids, and tombs of their ancient ancestors. You may even spot graffiti left by other tourists. Some just write their names and the date. Others write comments.

SEE A SCHOOL

Most children have no opportunity to learn to read and write, but some may be lucky enough to have a tutor or to learn from a scribe. The children who get an education are generally children whose fathers are scribes, administrators, or other members of the upper class. Some children of craftspeople may study reading and writing in the hopes of advancing to a higher class than their parents. Kids may also receive instruction in archery and horseback riding as preparation for becoming soldiers.

Starting in the Middle Kingdom, you may hear about schools, particularly for children of the nobles. By the New Kingdom, schools are

Colossal columns line the Great Hypostyle Hall in the Temple of Amun-Re at Karnak.

more common. You will not likely find girls in school—they learn household skills from their mothers. Boys, however, start school any time between the ages of five and ten, depending upon their level of maturity. They learn reading, writing, and arithmetic (sound familiar?). Like most activities in ancient Egypt, school takes place outdoors. There are no school textbooks, at least not until the later years.

Valuable papyrus is not as plentiful here as paper is at home. Kids write their lessons on ostraca (pieces of broken pottery) or on a limestone tablet that hangs from a cord for easy carrying. Pens are thin plant stalks chewed or pounded at one end to make a brush. Instead of ink, you'll get a solid chunk of black soot or red ocher. You must dip your brush in water and then moisten the coloring material. Make a mistake? No erasers or "White Out" here. Just lick away the mistake with your tongue. You will have to write down what the teacher says, copying and recopying. Even math is learned by copying examples, as there are no general rules for calculations yet.

SEE THE PYRAMIDS (BEING BUILT)

Here is your chance to solve one of the greatest mysteries of the world: How were the pyramids built? Sure, the locals have lots of time and lots of manpower. But let's face it—with no cutting tools, machinery, lifting

The step pyramid at Saqqara was built for the pharaoh Djoser in 2600 B.C.

Check out these facts on the Pyramid of Khufu:

Size of the base: 13.5 acres

Height: 480 feet

Number of limestone blocks: 2.3 million (92 million cubic feet)

Weight of each block: 2.5 tons

Measurement by which the sides of the base miss being a perfect square: 7 inches

Amount the north and south sides are off true parallel: 1 inch

Amount of error in aligning the sides to the compass directions (north, south, east, and west): less than $\frac{1}{10}$ of 1 degree

devices, or wheeled vehicles, the pyramids are quite an undertaking. Whatever you discover, you will find that the pyramid builders must take great care to make the sides exactly equal and the angles exactly right so that the sides meet at a point and the pyramid doesn't twist.

The kind of pyramid you see will depend upon when you travel. During the First Dynasty (3000 B.C.–2800 B.C.), all you will see are mastabas—flat mud-brick buildings that conceal underground burial chambers. If you go during the Third Dynasty (2675 B.C.–2625 B.C.), you

will see step pyramids. These structures are shaped like pyramids with giant steps leading up to the top. By the Fourth Dynasty (2625 B.C.–2500 B.C.), you will begin to see the smooth-sided pyramids. If you wait until the New Kingdom, you won't see any new pyramids at all. New Kingdom pharaohs decide that pyramids are like huge signs advertising where the tombs are. To protect their burial goods from grave robbers, they hide their tombs in the cliffs at Thebes.

Visit the Temple of Amun-Re at Karnak

If you go to Thebes, you can't miss this temple, on the east bank of the Nile. It is almost a city in itself, with elaborate entrances, roads lined with sphinxes, and sacred lakes. Although this complex is dedicated to the god Amun-Re, it houses temples built by a number of pharaohs.

At the north entrance to the temple, the pharaoh Amenhotep III created a chapel to Amun-Re and decorated it with bits of gold, malachite, and lapis lazuli. Not a humble person, Amenhotep also erected two enormous statues of himself near the beginning of the road linking Karnak with the Temple of Mut.

If you visit during the later part of the Nineteenth Dynasty (1292 B.C.–1190 B.C.) or later, look for the Great Hypostyle Hall. The hall is no small affair, measuring 338 feet by 170 feet—nearly the size of a football field. The floors are made of huge stone slabs, from which 134 columns rise to the stone beams that support the stone roof. This building was made to last! The columns are decorated with beautiful painted reliefs (sculptures that stand out from a flat background). If you are wondering how the locals could manage such enormous pieces of stone, look carefully and you will see that the columns are actually made of a series of half-disks, each three and one-half feet thick, stacked one pair on top of the other.

FESTIVALS

The locals are big on festivals and celebrations. There are sixty-five festivals on the official calendar, and individual villages often add more. Some festivals celebrate the full moon. Others honor the beginning of spring or the Nile's flood. Some are feast days connected with specific gods.

The Feast of Opet in Thebes can last for twenty-four days. It takes place when the Nile is nearing its highest point. One of the highlights is when the locals take the sacred statue of Amun from the temple at Karnak. They bring the statue by special barge to the temple at Luxor, where the pharaoh leads a procession to the temple. Crowds of spectators follow, pushing each other to get a glimpse of the pharaoh, high-ranking officials, and members of important families. The people want to be ready for the free food. Festivals feature massive quantities of food as well as singing, dancing, and partying that lasts for many days and nights.

The Temple of Amun-Re (facing page)

Where to Find Sports & Recreation

Nefertiti plays the board game senet, *which is based on beliefs of the Egyptian afterlife.*

Games

One of the most popular Egyptian pastimes is a board game called *senet*. It is a little like Parcheesi or Sorry, although the board has only three rows of ten squares. Players throw a set of sticks (instead of dice) and then move their pieces around the board. Some squares, like "water," are hazards, while others, such as "power," are good. The game symbolizes passing through the underworld, facing divine judgment, and being reborn in the afterlife.

Another popular game is *mehen,* which is played on a circular board. Players move their pieces from space to space in a spiral toward the center. You may be surprised to find that children never play board games, although they are popular among adults.

SPORTS

There are lots of sports in ancient Egypt. In one game, two kids climb onto the backs of two other kids and toss a ball back and forth. Another game you may see involves tossing a long wooden stick up in the air. Before the stick hits the ground, players try to hit it with another stick or club. Whoever hits their stick the farthest wins. You may see a game similar to bowling. Young people love to dance, perform acrobatics, and create balancing acts.

Boys and girls enjoy games. In one popular game, a boy gets on all fours and closes his eyes. Someone pokes him in the back, and he has to guess who has poked him. You may see a game called "jumping over the goose," where two boys sit facing each other with their legs and arms on top of each other. Another kid has to jump over this whole mess. Boys enjoy races and wrestling matches. Tug-of-war is also very popular, as is a game similar to arm wrestling.

Girls are particularly fond of ball games. In one game, girls ride piggyback on their partners while passing balls to each other. In another, girls stand in a group. Four girls clap their hands while two others toss and catch three balls in rotation. Girls also like to juggle.

HUNTING

The locals enjoy hunting for sport as well as for food. Some of the animals they hunt include wild cattle, gazelle, and ibex. Kings enjoy hunting lions. Ancient Egyptians hunt with bows and arrows and use throwing sticks to bring down ducks and other flying birds. In the early periods, they hunt hippopotamus with harpoons.

A terra-cotta (clay) "soul house," or model buried with the dead, shows the layout of typical ancient Egyptian housing.

WHERE TO STAY

PRIVATE HOMES

The main purpose of housing in ancient Egypt is not shelter from rain but shelter from the sun. The buildings have thick brick walls and few windows. Some homes even have "air conditioners"—openings on the roof designed to catch the wind and air out the house.

If you stay in a working family's home, you will find it rather small. It will probably have four rooms. At the front will be a windowless room facing the street. Behind this you will find the living room. This is where the family eats, sleeps, works, and entertains company. You may find cushioned couches and wooden chairs. Behind this are usually two smaller rooms. One is the kitchen, and the other may be an extra bedroom or just a storage area. Looking for more space? Try the roof. The locals consider it part of the house, so there'll be a stairway leading to it. The roof acts as the front yard, backyard, and garden, especially in the crowded cities.

You will find sleeping somewhat of a challenge. The beds are higher at the head than at the foot, so there is a footboard to keep you from sliding off. There are no pillows. Instead you will have a wooden headrest. If you need light, look for the small pottery lamps filled with oil. The wicks are twisted rags soaked in tallow. They give off a warm, yellow light.

If you are lucky enough to stay with a noble, you will find more comfortable accommodations. The noble's villa is probably built of brick or wood. It may have a pool and garden. You will find a reception hall when you first

Hot Hint

You may find that the furnishings people put in their tombs are nicer than the ones they use in their homes. The furnishings help ensure a good time in the afterlife.

This illustration, created by a French artist in the 1800s, shows a brightly painted courtyard in an ancient Egyptian palace.

enter. Behind that is a sort of great room where the family hangs out. It will have a built-in sofa and a place for a fire on cool nights. There is little furniture, but wall hangings, woven mats, and painted columns make the inside bright and pretty. The bedrooms are in a separate area and some even have their own sitting areas. You will see a platform in each bedroom. There will be a mattress—a wooden frame and springs of cord or leather—to put on top for sleeping.

You will find the bathroom facilities impressive compared to other ancient destinations, which usually have no bathroom facilities at all. The toilet is a seat set on a stack of bricks in a little walled-off area.

Underneath is a pot that a servant or slave will empty and replace. There are no bathtubs, as the locals find sitting in stagnant water disgusting. But you can take a shower by standing on a stone slab and pouring water over yourself. Wealthy folks have servants to pour for them. The water drains out through a hole in the floor, generally into a container that has to be bailed out by hand. Don't be surprised if you see clay, brass, or copper pipes and even, perhaps, stoppers for keeping the water in a basin. The locals are very clean. Some, especially the priests, bathe several times a day. Servants bathe, shave, and make up the hair of upper-class people every day, even while traveling. Poor folks bathe in the river.

SIDE TRIP TRIVIA If you visit Mohenjo-Daro, a city in the Indus River Valley in ancient India, between 2500 B.C. and 1500 B.C., you will find that the houses are packed close together. This has led to a remarkable invention—the sewage system. The houses in Mohenjo-Daro actually have bathrooms and toilets with drains. The drains carry water through pipes under the streets to disposal areas outside the city. They even have manhole covers so workers can climb down to fix clogs.

The locals leave wastewater to drain into the ground, and they dump garbage any old place. Birds, dogs, rats, and other animals carry off what they like. The rest just rots in the sun, although the heat and dryness of the climate help keep the stench down. The government, particularly in cities such as Thebes, tries to get people to use a specified dumping area outside of town. Even so, many people just toss the mess wherever it's handy when no one is looking. Deir el-Medina has trash collection, but this is unusual.

PUBLIC ACCOMMODATIONS

You will not find any hotels or other commercial places to stay. When the locals travel to festivals or other sites, they generally just sleep out in the open and bring their own food or scrounge what they can. Important people, such as those on government assignments, get special treatment. Pharaohs command local officials to find lodging and food for the VIPs and their fellow travelers.

If you can get a letter of permission from a top official or a royal family member, you will be allowed into the royal palace. In ancient Egypt, where farmable land is so valuable, the pharaohs take as much space as they like for their own homes. The palace has huge rooms. In the New Kingdom, each room has vividly painted walls, floors, and ceilings. It's hard to tell what's real, with painted birds flying across the ceiling, columns made to look like plants, and walls painted with leaping animals, strolling court ladies, and kneeling prisoners. You may have to look twice before stepping onto a floor painted to look like a pool, complete with fish, water lilies, and ducks swimming on the surface. You will find courtyards, gardens, and spacious chambers, including both private apartments for the royal family and public areas such as audience halls.

What to Eat

Household slaves prepare beer and bread.

Hold the Ketchup, Hold the Mayo

Unfortunately, ancient Egypt doesn't have any restaurants, so you will
have to buy food at the market and find someone to prepare it for you.
The food you will get most often is bread. Although kings and nobles
have many different kinds of bread to choose from, you will find mainly
flatbread. As far as vegetables, you will find lentils, fava beans, peas, leeks,
lettuce, cucumbers, radishes, and onions. You will also see seeds and tu-
bers (a kind of root), particularly the tuber from nut grass. You may also
eat the shoots, leaves, or roots of several plants. You will not find any
sugar here, but honey is used to sweeten food, especially cakes. Dates,
figs, melons, pomegranates, apricots, and grapes are popular fruits.

Most folks can't afford meat often, although you will see it on festival days. The locals keep sheep, goats, cattle, and pigs. Aside from farm

71

animals, you will find game such as wild cattle, hartebeest, deer, hares, gazelle, antelope, jackals, and desert cats. The locals also hunt wild birds, then preserve them by salting.

Meat is so valuable that when butchers kill oxen, they collect the blood and use it for food. Animal fat is considered quite a luxury. When people serve meat, they often spit-roast it whole—even the oxen. You will see women cutting up beef for boiling, too. The locals consider the legs the best part.

You will also find fish, especially tilapia, perch, and catfish. Fish are especially easy to catch after the floods, when they can be scooped up in nets. You may see them (or rather, smell them) salted and laid out to dry in the sun on the roofs of houses. The locals also smoke the fish. You may find turtle and mussels from the Nile.

Try some fresh grape juice while you are here. Although much of it goes to make wine, grape juice is readily available from vineyards, which are generally nearby. Ancient Egyptians enjoy juice from other fruits such as pomegranates and figs. You will also find milk. The main beverages here, however, are beer and wine.

A cow is sacrificed as an offering to the gods. Very few ancient Egyptians eat beef on a regular basis.

MEALTIME

If you watch while the women of the house prepare your meal, you will find that everything happens on a lower level than it does at home. There are no cabinets, so cooks line up pots and jars on the floor along

FOODS TO TRY

- Ful (pronounced "fool")—a bean dish that is very popular with the locals

- Chickpeas and lotus seeds flavored with marjoram, coriander, and dill

- Honey cakes

- Gazelle meat basted with honey

- Onions—they are mild and of excellent flavor

FOODS TO TRY,
at your own risk

- A dish containing lumps of fat in radish oil seasoned with cumin. You may find juniper berries bobbing in the oil.

- Dishes, such as black pudding, made with fresh blood

the kitchen walls. There are no countertops, so women prepare the food on or near the floor while squatting on the ground. The oven is a pottery container approximately thirty inches high. It has a drawer near the floor for the coals and a drawer on top for the food. When you eat a meal, you will sit on a stool or mat at a small table.

If you eat at the home of a wealthy person, your host will treat you in style. A servant will greet you, provide you with water for washing before dinner, and generally tend to your needs. Don't be concerned if the servant starts rubbing a sweet-scented ointment on your head—this is a token of welcome.

Egyptian slaves press grapes in a vat to make wine.

Graceful dancers and talented musicians entertain guests at banquets.

Wealthy locals love to hold lavish banquets for their friends and relatives. They will serve rich foods, such as butter and cheese, seldom enjoyed by common folk. Nobles have beef, mutton, and birds such as goose and duck. You will also find that they season the food with herbs and spices such as rosemary, cumin, parsley, cinnamon, and mustard.

If you are invited to a banquet, you will find not only lots of food, but also music, dancing, clapping, and finger snapping. Your host will greet you warmly and drape you in flower petals and scented wreaths of flowers. There will probably be a harp and perhaps some small drums or a tambourine. If you visit late enough (Eighteenth Dynasty and beyond), you may even see lyres, oboes, and lutes. You may see hand-shaped ivory clappers that players knock together to make sound.

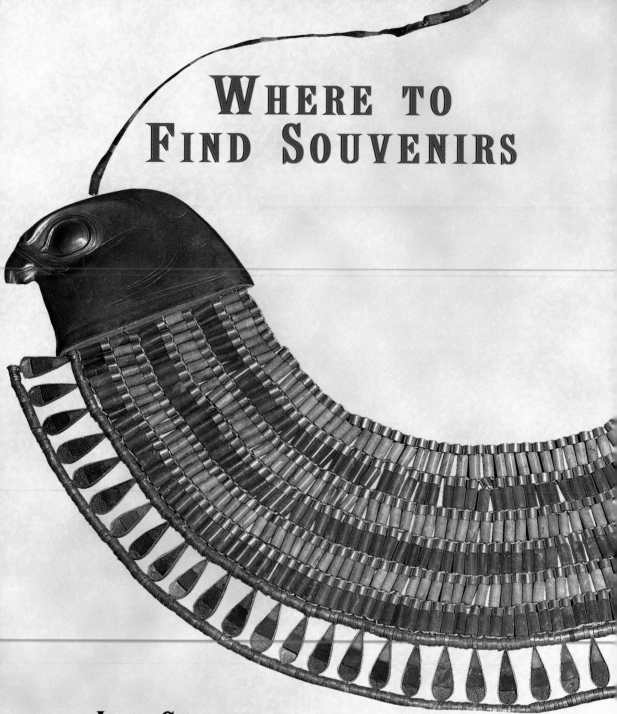

Where to Find Souvenirs

Arts, Crafts, & Other Delights

If you like jewelry, ancient Egypt is the place for you. There is probably no other destination with finer jewelry. You may be surprised to see gold in various colors in addition to yellow. Gold often contains other metals, such as silver, copper, or iron, which can change its color to gray, reddish-brown, or even pink.

76

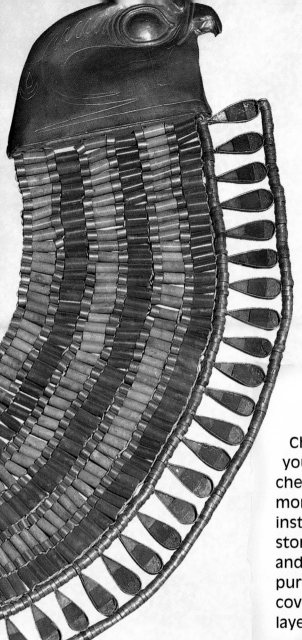

This collar is a fine example of ancient Egyptian jewelry. Gold, carnelian (a reddish stone), and feldspar (a stone often bluish or greenish in color) decorate the piece.

Hot Hint

Check objects carefully before you buy. Artists often make cheaper materials look more valuable. For instance, what looks like stone may just be pottery, and what seems to be pure gold may be plaster covered with only a thin layer of gold.

Not only do Egyptians have remarkable supplies of gold, but they have also developed ways to use it to its full advantage. They can do almost anything with gold that modern jewelers can do—including making chains and creating delicate open designs called filigree. Unfortunately, gold is generally affordable only for those of noble birth; copper is for the common folk.

You will also see a lot of faience. To make faience, artisans grind quartz, mix it with glue, and mold it into shapes. They can then glaze it and make it resemble gems or stones such as turquoise. Jewelry made with faience is inexpensive and quite popular.

BEST BUYS IN ANCIENT EGYPT

Necklaces—look for ones made with rose-pink gold or with pendants containing blue lapis, red jasper, green feldspar, lavender amethyst, orange-red carnelian, or purplish-red garnets.

Cosmetic boxes—these may be filled with small combs, pots of ointments, and polished metal mirrors with handles carved into the shapes of animals or flowers.

Game boards—look for senet boards made of ebony and ivory, boards with peg holes for playing a game called hounds and jackals (some may be shaped like a hippopotamus), or circular mehen boards (some of the playing pieces look like reclining lions).

Headrests—look for ones with carvings or interesting colors. Some even contain gold.

Pottery—look for pottery made near Qena in Upper Egypt from a special light-colored clay.

How to Stay Safe & Healthy

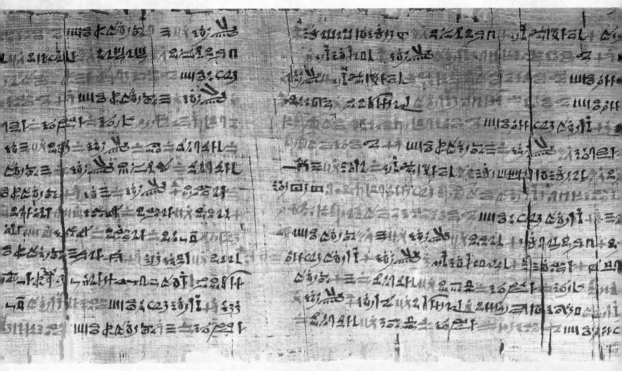

This papyrus, dating from around 1200 B.C., is an ancient Egyptian medical text.

Take Some Cow Bile & Call Me in the Morning

Doctors are of a high social rank. You will find that doctors specialize in certain parts of the body, as they do in modern times. At home you might go to an ear, nose, and throat specialist. In ancient Egypt, they have doctors of the head and teeth, doctors of the feet, and even doctors of the belly. Physicians at the royal palace have even more important titles. One you might not envy is the Keeper of the Royal Rectum.

The doctor is called *swnw* (SOO-noo). Like a modern doctor, he or she will ask you questions about your condition, feel your pulse, palpate your body (press to feel for abnormalities inside), and examine secretions such as mucus or urine. If you have a wound, don't be surprised

*Ancient Egyptian surgical knives
made from pounded bronze*

if the doctor smells it. If you have a broken arm, the doctor will wrap it in palm-fiber lint and set it with tree-bark splints.

If you visit during the Middle Kingdom or later, your doctor may refer to medical texts that describe individual cases, symptoms, findings from physical examinations, and whether the condition is curable, treatable, or untreatable. Treatments and prescriptions are listed as well.

DISEASES, DISASTERS, & OTHER ANNOYANCES

You will find that the locals do not separate science, religion, and magic. They blame bad spirits and angry dead people for disease. They believe that to stay healthy, one must be protected against these forces. Therefore, they use magic amulets and chants as well as medicines and medical treatments. The locals have no understanding of the actual causes or prevention of infection. Bacteria and their role in disease won't be discovered until the A.D. 1700s.

Now Hear This

If thou examinest a man having a gaping wound in his shoulder, its flesh being laid back and its sides separated, while he suffers with swelling [in] his shoulder blade, thou shouldst palpate his wound. Shouldst thou find its gash separated from its sides in his wound, as a roll of linen is unrolled, [and] it is painful when he raises his arm on account of it, thou shouldst draw together for him his gash with stitching.

—*the* Edwin Smith Surgical Papyrus

Many locals are sick or in pain quite often. For one thing, parasites, including hookworm and roundworm, are often found in soil. Ancient Egyptians catch parasites easily because they walk barefoot through fields and ditches and bathe in the river. Insect, animal, and even human bites are common. So are eye problems—especially ophthalmia, a serious kind of inflammation. Flies, as well as contact with an infected person, can spread viral trachoma (a common cause of blindness) and other eye infections. Other common complaints include ear infection, headache, indigestion, and rheumatism. Egyptians might also catch pneumonia, smallpox, tuberculosis, and polio.

The main problem which the locals suffer from is toothache. Ancient Egyptians start out with good teeth, but the coarse grain in the bread, combined with bits of sand and even gravel from the stones used to mill the grain, quickly wears down teeth. Worn-out teeth can get infected. Without effective treatment available, infections eventually cause death.

Doctors generally give medicines mixed with liquids such as milk, water, or beer. They also prescribe various ointments. Some doctors feel that the body will reject a disease if the medicine is so awful, so disgusting, so absolutely. . . well, you get the idea. One medicine the locals give sick kids is a skinned mouse. Which must be swallowed. Whole. Common ingredients for medicines include animal blood, fat, bones, and organs; insects; and plant materials. So if you think medicines at home smell bad, wait until you get a whiff of salves made from ingredients such as sandal leather, soot, cow bile, and human or animal excrement.

Other than disease, the problems you are most likely to encounter are related to the rise and fall of the Nile. Flood levels are unpredictable. The river can rise much higher than usual, destroying local villages. Or it can flood too little, causing food shortages later. You should also know that during the inundation, small towns can become islands for weeks or even months, which may put a damper (get it? *damp*-er) on your travel plans. During times of drought, you may find outbreaks of disease and general mayhem. It is even possible that the locals will resort to cannibalism.

WATCH FOR WARS

There are periods, such as the New Kingdom, when military conflicts occur practically every year. Most of these battles are outside Egypt in the foreign lands of Syria, Canaan, Nubia, or Libya, where they are unlikely to cause you any problems. However, there are times when conflicts break out, invaders attack, and citizens—not just soldiers—are expected to help defend Egypt.

A panel from a chest buried with King Tutankhamen shows an Egyptian victory over the Nubians.

Ancient Egyptians use weapons such as these in battle against their enemies.

If you observe a battle during the early periods, you will find the techniques and strategies rather primitive. Without firearms, the troops must get close enough to fire arrows. The soldiers advance until they are face to face. Then they begin stabbing, clubbing, and hacking at each other until one side runs away. This is an ugly affair, as there is no body armor and most soldiers are dressed only in kilts.

LAW & ORDER

The locals have quite a commitment to justice. In theory at least, even the lowliest peasant can go to court and, if the verdict seems unfair, can appeal to a supreme court. In extreme cases, the plaintiff can appeal to the pharaoh. In reality peasants aren't treated quite as respectfully. Nevertheless, the locals are quick to take petty arguments over land, water rights, and other issues to court. They accuse each other of all kinds of things and rely on a judge to sort it all out.

You won't see police officers. A group called the *medjay* guards the frontiers and cemeteries. They also chase down criminals, following tips provided by the locals. Most people avoid contact with the law if they can. Interrogation (questioning of suspects) generally involves beating the suspects and twisting their arms and legs in torture devices.

Punishments are considerably worse. A common sentence is one hundred strokes with a stick, sometimes with an order to wound the offender. Authorities may send a criminal to work in the mines or quarries for various terms, according to the severity of the crime. Or convicts may be permanently banished to a desert outpost. Mutilation is a common punishment. For example, a person who lies in court may have his nose and ears cut off.

One of the most serious crimes here is tomb robbing. It often takes a whole team to pull it off. Stonemasons cut through the walls, water carriers help tunnel and then haul out the loot, and metalworkers melt down the plunder. Someone must drive the getaway car, er, boat. To make it easy, sometimes the robbers simply set fire to the contents of the tomb and then collect the gold, which doesn't burn. The robbers often cut out the eyes of the figures drawn on the walls of the tombs so that the painted people don't witness the crime. Tomb robbers who are caught are generally executed. The good news is that the death penalty is relatively rare, and only the king can hand it down. In some cases, particularly if the offender is of high social standing, the king may let him choose between execution and suicide.

For the most part, you will not have to worry much about crime. In large cities such as Thebes, you will have to take care at night, for thieves can lurk in some areas. You should also avoid traveling alone outside cities.

WHO'S WHO IN ANCIENT EGYPT

RAMSES II

Ramses II takes the throne in 1279 B.C. and begins a sixty-six-year reign during which he directs the construction of palaces, temples, and several larger-than-life statues. Not one to be modest, Ramses II orders the carving of the Colossus of Memphis, a twenty-four-foot, seven-inch statue of himself.

Ramses II was the last of Egypt's great warrior-pharaohs. His most famous battle occurred at Kadesh in Syria, when enemy troops cut him off from his men. According to an inscription written by Ramses II, he charged the enemy in his chariot,

Back TO THE FUTURE

You may think, having heard so much about him, that Tutankhamen is an important ruler. Actually, the only reason he is so famous in modern times is that his tomb was one of very few to be discovered intact. (He only ruled for nine or ten years—from the age of nine to about eighteen.) Other rulers are much more important. Their tombs were plundered by robbers, however, so they are less known to modern people.

drove the warriors into a river, and captured twenty-five hundred enemy chariots single-handedly. Of course, we only have his word for it.

HATSHEPSUT

If you visit between about 1504 B.C. and 1458 B.C., try to meet Hatshepsut. Around 1518 B.C., her father, Pharaoh Thutmose I, dies. Hatshepsut marries her half-brother, Thutmose II, following a common custom for keeping power within the ruling family. But that's where her interest in following the common custom stops. She governs with her husband/half-brother, taking an equal (some say greater) role in ruling the land. When Thutmose II dies, his son Thutmose III, by a different wife, would normally inherit the throne. But Thutmose III is too young to rule, so Hatshepsut acts as regent (stand-in ruler). After a couple of years, she declares herself king of Egypt and starts wearing men's clothes—even the false beard commonly worn by pharaohs. She launches extensive trade expeditions, sponsors building projects, and directs military campaigns.

PEPI II

This guy is worth visiting, if only to see someone who has never heard of early retirement. Pepi (and that's a good name for him) comes to the throne during the Sixth Dynasty at the age of six and rules for, get this, ninety-four years. Keep in mind, most of his fellow ancient Egyptians don't make it to forty.

AHHOTEP

Around 1600 B.C., when the locals in Thebes revolt against the Hyksos control of Egypt, Ahhotep is married to Seqenenre II, Egyptian ruler of Thebes. Ahhotep and Seqenenre have children, including two sons, Kamose and Ahmose. Seqenenre dies fighting the Hyksos, so Kamose takes the throne. Kamose destroys the Hyksos power in Middle Egypt, but his reign is short, possibly because he is killed in battle. His younger brother, Ahmose, is too young to rule, so Ahhotep steps in. She keeps up the pressure on the Hyksos for more than ten years, until Ahmose is able to rule on his own.

For her military valor, Queen Ahhotep receives a special decoration—a necklace with three pendants shaped like gold flies. Each fly is nearly as large as your hand, and the necklace contains more than half a pound of gold. The Flies of Valor are given by the pharaoh for bravery on the battlefield.

AKHENATON

When Amenhotep III dies in 1352 B.C., his son, Amenhotep IV, takes the throne. After six years, he changes his name from Amenhotep (Amun Is Grateful) to Akhenaton (Serviceable to the Aten—or Aton—the god of the sun disk). This is more than just a simple name change. Together with his wife Nefertiti, Akhenaton rejects the locals' belief in Amun, the creator and king of gods, in favor of Aten, the sun god of the city of Heliopolis. He creates a new city, names it Akhetaten (Horizon of the Sun Disk), and declares it the new capital. He starts erecting shrines to Aten in Thebes. At the shrines, you will see Aten portrayed as a disk with rays that end with human hands.

Not everyone is pleased with Akhenaton's changes, and many continue to worship the old gods. Akhenaton sends representatives to close temples, destroy images of the gods, and collect money for the new capital. They even cut the names of the other deities from the walls of tombs and change the names of anyone whose name contains the word Amun.

Akhenaton hangs in for seventeen years, while the Hittites of nearby Asia Minor threaten Egypt's northern borders. Egypt itself goes into a decline. The next pharaoh, Tutankhaten, abandons the capital of Akhetaten. He changes his name to Tutankhamen, reflecting the return to the worship of Amun.

Preparing for the Trip

Measuring with Cubits

You can use your body to measure spaces, just as the ancient Egyptians did. Ask a friend to help you hold one end of a piece of string to your elbow and the other end to the tip of your middle finger. Cut the string. You have a one-cubit measuring tool.

Use your string to measure the distance around your classroom. Compare your results to those of your classmates. Did everyone get the same number? What might happen if you and your classmates tried to build a pyramid? How could you make sure your measurements stayed accurate?

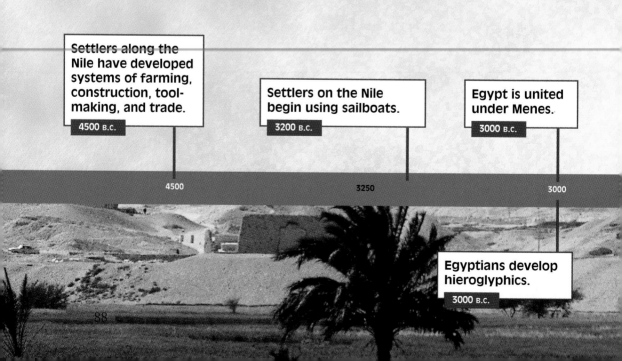

Settlers along the Nile have developed systems of farming, construction, tool-making, and trade.
4500 B.C.

Settlers on the Nile begin using sailboats.
3200 B.C.

Egypt is united under Menes.
3000 B.C.

4500

3250

3000

Egyptians develop hieroglyphics.
3000 B.C.

Ful Medames

Ancient Egyptians love this tasty bean stew, and it's popular in modern-day Egypt, too. In fact, it's Egypt's national dish. You might want to ask an adult for help.

⅓ cup olive oil
2–3 cloves garlic, minced
1½ teaspoon ground cumin
1 teaspoon ground black pepper
2 19-ounce cans fava beans

4 tablespoons chopped onion
1 lemon, quartered
4 hard-boiled eggs, chopped
4–8 pieces of pita bread

Heat the olive oil in a pot or large saucepan. Sauté the garlic until soft, 1 to 2 minutes. Add the cumin and black pepper. Cook 1 to 2 minutes more. Add the beans with their liquid. Bring the mixture to a boil, then lower the heat and simmer 20 to 30 minutes until the liquid is thick. You may want to mash the mixture a bit to thicken the juice.

Put the remaining ingredients on the table in bowls or on plates. Serve the ful in bowls. Sprinkle on eggs and onions, squeeze lemon juice over the dish, and accompany your meal with pita bread. (**Serves 4**)

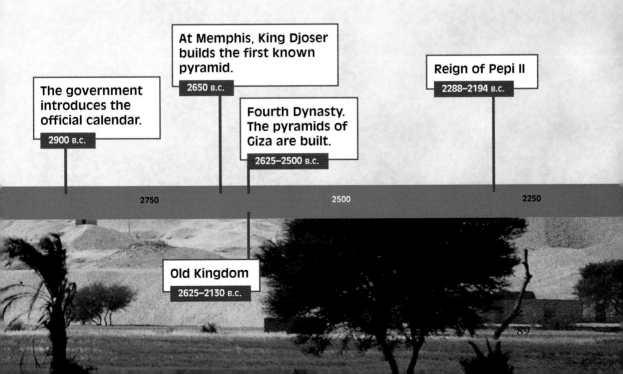

At Memphis, King Djoser builds the first known pyramid.
2650 B.C.

Reign of Pepi II
2288–2194 B.C.

The government introduces the official calendar.
2900 B.C.

Fourth Dynasty. The pyramids of Giza are built.
2625–2500 B.C.

2750   2500   2250

Old Kingdom
2625–2130 B.C.

89

GLOSSARY

barter: to purchase items by trading them for other goods

classical period: an era when a country's culture, wealth, and political achievements reach a high point

dynasty: a period of rule by a single family or group

hieratic writing: a script based on simplified forms of hieroglyphic pictures

hieroglyphics: a written language that uses pictures to represent words

inundation: a flood, such as the annual flooding of the Nile River

irrigation: bringing water to dry farmland

pharaoh: the Egyptian king, who functioned as the head of state, the chief religious official, and the highest judge in the country

scribe: a person trained in reading, writing, and mathematics. Scribes worked as administrators, record keepers, and overseers.

vizier: a high-ranking officer of the pharaoh's court

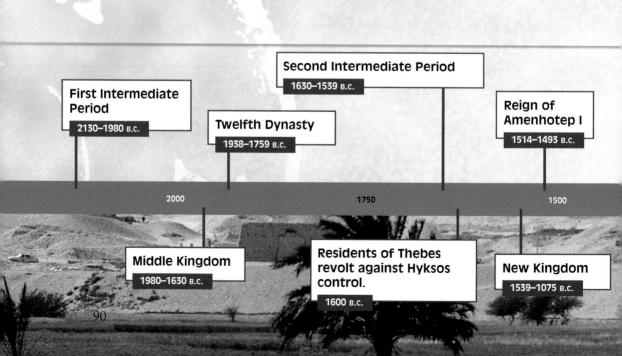

First Intermediate Period
2130–1980 B.C.

Second Intermediate Period
1630–1539 B.C.

Twelfth Dynasty
1938–1759 B.C.

Reign of Amenhotep I
1514–1493 B.C.

2000

1750

1500

Middle Kingdom
1980–1630 B.C.

Residents of Thebes revolt against Hyksos control.
1600 B.C.

New Kingdom
1539–1075 B.C.

Pronunciation Guide

Ahhotep	AH-hoh-tehp
Ahmose	AH-mohs
Akhenaton	ahk-NAH-tuhn
Amenhotep	ah-muhn-HOH-tehp
Hatshepsut	haht-SHEHP-soot
hieratic	hy-RAT-ihk
hieroglyphics	hy-roh-GLIHF-ihks
Hyksos	HIHK-sahs
Kamose	KAH-mohs
Menes	MEE-neez
Nefertiti	neh-fuhr-TEE-tee
Pepi	PAY-pee
pharaoh	FEHR-oh
Ramses	RAM-seez
Seqenenre	say-keh-NEHN-ray
Thutmose	thoot-MOH-suh
Tutankhamen	too-tahn-KAH-muhn
Tutankhaten	too-tahn-KAH-tuhn

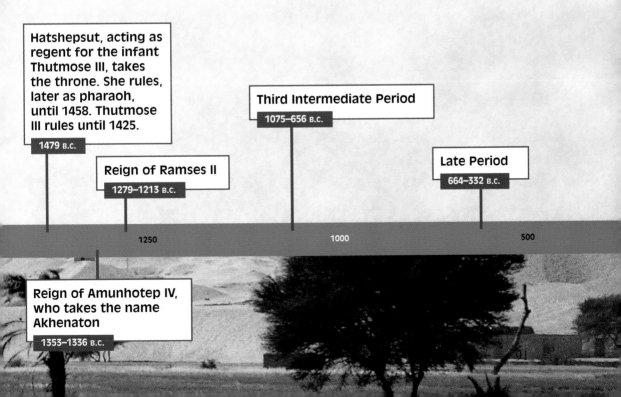

Hatshepsut, acting as regent for the infant Thutmose III, takes the throne. She rules, later as pharaoh, until 1458. Thutmose III rules until 1425.

1479 B.C.

Third Intermediate Period

1075–656 B.C.

Reign of Ramses II

1279–1213 B.C.

Late Period

664–332 B.C.

1250

1000

500

Reign of Amunhotep IV, who takes the name Akhenaton

1353–1336 B.C.

91

FURTHER READING

Books

Barghusen, Joan D. *Daily Life in Ancient and Modern Cairo.* Minneapolis: Runestone Press, 2001.

Egypt in Pictures. Minneapolis: Lerner Publications Company, 1998.

Guy, J. A. *Egyptian Life.* Hauppage, NY: Barrons Juveniles, 1998.

McNeill, Sarah, and Sarah Howarth. *Ancient Egyptian People.* Brookfield, CT: Millbrook Press, 1997.

Morley, Jacqueline. *How Would You Survive as an Ancient Egyptian?* Danbury, CT: Franklin Watts, 1996.

Steedman, Scott, and Deni Bown. *DK Pockets: Ancient Egypt.* New York: Dorling Kindersley, 1996.

Internet Sites

Ancient Egypt Webquest
<http://users.massed.net/~mdurant/AncientEgyptWebquest.htm>

British Museum
<http://www.ancientegypt.co.uk>

Carnegie Museum of Natural History
<http://www.clpgh.org/cmnh/exhibits/egypt>

Nova Online Mysteries of the Nile
<http://www.pbs.org/wgbh/nova/egypt>

BIBLIOGRAPHY

Casson, Lionel, and the editors of Time-Life Books. *Ancient Egypt.* New York: Time Incorporated, 1965.

Casson, Lionel. *Travel in the Ancient World.* Baltimore: The Johns Hopkins University Press, 1994.

Grimal, Nicolas. *A History of Ancient Egypt.* New York: Barnes & Noble Books, 1998.

James, Peter, and Nick Thorpe. *Ancient Inventions.* New York: Ballantine Books, 1994.

Janssen, Rosalind M., and Jac. J. Janssen. *Growing Up in Ancient Egypt.* London: The Rubicon Press, 1991.

Majno, Guido. *The Healing Hand: Man and Wound in the Ancient World.* Cambridge, MA: Harvard University Press, 1991.

Mertz, Barbara. *Red Land, Black Land: Daily Life in Ancient Egypt.* New York: Dodd, Mead & Company, 1978.

Reader's Digest. *Everyday Life Through the Ages.* London: Reader's Digest, 1992.

Riefstahl, Elizabeth. *Thebes in the Time of Amunhotep III.* Norman, OK: University of Oklahoma Press, 1964.

Romer, John. *Ancient Lives: Daily Life in Egypt of the Pharaohs.* New York: Holt, Rinehart and Winston, 1984.

Silverman, David P., ed. *Ancient Egypt.* New York: Oxford University Press, 1997.

Sprague de Camp, L. *Great Cities of the Ancient World.* New York: Doubleday & Company, Inc., 1972.

What Life Was Like on the Banks of the Nile: Egypt 3050–30 B.C. Alexandria, VA: Time-Life Books, 1996.

INDEX

Osiris, 40–42, 46, 51

paper making, 28
peasants, 37
Pepi II, 86
Peret (growing season), 14
pharaohs, 23–24, 35–36, 43–44, 62, 70,
    85–87
political structure, 35
population, 35
Pyramid of Khufu, 61
pyramids, 7, 10, 60–62

queens, 36. *See also* Nefertiti

Ramses II, 46, 85–86
Red Land, 14, 31, 39
Rosetta Stone, 8

scribes, 17–19, 37, 43, 59
Second Intermediate Period (1630
    B.C.–1539 B.C.), 11
Shemu (season of drought), 14, 30
slavery, 39, 74
social structure, 35
souvenirs, 76–78
sports and recreation, 64–65
sundials, 16

taxes, 35
Temple of Amun-Re, 42, 59, 62–63
temples, 42–43
Thebes, 11, 22–24, 31, 62–63, 69
Third Dynasty (2675 B.C.–2625 B.C.),
    61–62
Third Intermediate Period (1075
    B.C.–656 B.C.), 11
time measurement, 9–10, 15–17
timeline, 88–89
Tiy, 36
transportation, 29–31
Tutankhamen, 82, 85, 87
Twelfth Dynasty (1938 B.C.–1759 B.C.),
    11

Upper Egypt, 10, 13–14, 23, 24

Valley of the Kings, 21, 23

wars, 82–83
Window of Appearances, 36
women, 38

ABOUT THE AUTHOR

Nancy Day is the author of nine books and forty-five articles for young people. She loves to read and is fascinated with the idea of time travel, which she says is "actually history in a great disguise." Her interest in time travel inspired the Passport to History series. Nancy Day lives with her husband, son, and two cats in a house that was built in 1827—before the Civil War. She often imagines what it would be like to go back in time to meet the ship-builder who once lived there.

Acknowledgments for Quoted Material p. 17, as quoted by Rosalind M. Janssen and Jac. J. Janssen, *Growing Up in Ancient Egypt* (London: The Rubicon Press, 1991); p. 23, as quoted by Elizabeth Riefstahl, *Thebes in the Time of Amunhotep III* (Normal, OK: University of Oklahoma Press, 1964); p. 81, as quoted by Guido Majno, *The Healing Hand: Man and Wound in the Ancient World* (Cambridge, MA: Harvard University Press, 1991).

Photo Acknowledgments The images in this book are used with the permission of: Museo Civico Archeologico, Bologna, p. 2; © Kenneth Garrett, pp. 6–7, 51, 64; © Drs. A. A. M. Van der Heyden, p. 10; © Erich Lessing/Art Resource, NY, pp. 12–13, 21, 27, 30–31, 35, 38, 39, 40, 42, 45, 54 (bottom), 55, 62, 66, 72–73, 83, 85 (both), 88–89, 90–91; © Gianni Dagli Orti/Corbis, pp. 16, 26, 33, 44, 54 (top), 68, 71, 74; © R. Sheridan/ Ancient Art & Architecture Collection, Ltd., p. 17; © Claudia Adams/Root Resources, pp. 18, 48; © Roger Wood/Corbis, p. 25; Dr. Stephen Derfler, pp. 28, 75; © Alinari/Art Resources, NY, p. 29; © Archivo Iconografico, S. A./Corbis, pp. 32, 76–77; © Bojan Brecelj/Corbis, p. 34; © Giraudon/Art Resource, NY, pp. 40–41, 52, 82; © Scala/Art Resource, NY, pp. 36–37, 46, 47, 58, 87; The British Museum, p. 49; © Nimatallah/Art Resource, NY, p. 50; AKG London, p. 56; © Werner Forman/Art Resource, NY, p. 57; © Carmen Redondo/Corbis, pp. 60–61; Chester Beatty Library, Dublin/Bridgeman Art Library, p. 79; Art Resource, NY, p. 80; Brooklyn Museum of Art, NY/Charles Edwin Wilbour Fund/Bridgeman Art Library, p. 86. Front cover: © Erich Lessing/Art Resource, NY (both).